STEAM IN KENT AND EAST

COMPILED AND PHOTOGRAPHED BY

DENNIS C. OVENDEN

INTRODUCTION

The photographs in this album were taken during the period 1956–1962, mainly on the former South Eastern Railway lines in Kent. This represents no antipathy on my part to the London, Chatham and Dover Railway (as was the case with the S.E.R. management in the last century) but rather force of circumstances.

Until 1961, when I acquired my own transport, time constraints resulted in a high percentage of my pictures being obtained within easy reach of my home at Hamstreet, and at Ashford, where I worked. Ashford was a very busy junction and a great variety of locomotives could be seen there. It is, perhaps, unusual for a junction of its importance in that all lines radiating from there – to Margate via Canterbury, London via Maidstone East, and to Hastings – are still open for passenger traffic, although the Hastings line has had its share of closure threats over the last twenty years.

From 1961, when I was able to widen the sphere of my activities, the Westerham and the delightfully rural Hawkhurst branches (both closed in that year) are represented here.

Also included are photographs from the former L.B.&S.C.R. lines in the lovely countryside around Groombridge and Eridge, where there was a good deal of steam activity some time after electrification reached most of Kent.

I would like to express my sincere thanks to the Public Relations Dept of B.R. Southern Region for granting me permits for lineside photography, without which I would have been unable to obtain many of my pictures.

Dennis C. Ovenden, Langley, Kent, 1990

FRONT COVER
Ashford – August 18th 1959. An up freight passes under the magnificent semaphore gantry hauled by class N No 31871.

INSIDE FRONT COVER
Ham Street and Orlestone – August 6th 1961. Two contrasting 0–6–0s. Class Q1 No 33028, piloted by class C No 31004, working hard up the 1 in 100 gradient with an engineering department train.

INSIDE BACK COVER
Cranbrook – April 22nd 1961. The Hawkhurst branch in its last year. On a showery day the 9.07am Paddock Wood–Hawkhurst train is leaving with class H No 31533 in charge.

BACK COVER
Groombridge – June 16th 1962. The 8.02am Victoria to Tunbridge Wells West train approaches, headed by B.R. class 4 2–6–4T No 80150.

THIS PAGE
Ruckinge Crossing – August 20th 1961. The 6.50am (Sundays) Hastings to Ashford train near the top of the 1 in 100 gradient up from Romney Marsh, headed by class N1 No 31880. Note the signal protecting the crossing on the wrong side, to enable easier vision for trains approaching round the left hand curve beyond the overbridge in the background.

Copyright D. C. Ovenden 1990.
Design by South Anglia Productions Studio.
Published by South Anglia Productions, 26 Rainham Way, Frinton-on-Sea, Essex CO13 9NS
ISBN 1 871277 07 8
Printed in England by The Lavenham Press Ltd.

No 34088 "213 SQUADRON", of the same class, passing Knockholt with a down boat-train. September 5th 1957.

Class H 0-4-4T No 31308 stands at Westerham with the 12.25pm train for Dunton Green. This branch was closed in the month after this picture was taken. The coaches are Maunsell push/pull set No 610. September 9th 1961.

Class L 4–4–0 No 31771 arriving at Tonbridge with a train from Redhill. The coaches are an ex-S.E.&C.R. "Birdcage" set. April 20th 1957.

Ex-L.B.&S.C.R. class E4 0–6–2T No 32578 leaving Tonbridge yard with a down freight. June 1st 1957.

Class C 0-6-0 No 31113 at Ashford with a freight train bound for the Maidstone line. January 6th 1960.

"Schools" class 4-4-0 No 30930 "RADLEY" arriving at Ashford with a train from Charing Cross. Work is being carried out on a connection with track

The 12.42pm stopping train for Tonbridge leaving Ashford double-headed by class N 2–6–0 No 31836 and class L 4–4–0 No 31766. April 24th 1959.

The 12.42pm stopping train for Tonbridge leaving Ashford headed by class L 4–4–0 No 31768. A class C 0–6–0 is stopped at the down signals with a freight train. April 28th 1959.

B.R. class 2 2–6–2T No 84021 waits to leave Ashford with a Maidstone East to Margate train. June 6th 1959.

"King Arthur" class 4–6–0 No 30806 "SIR GALLERON" at Ashford with a down freight train. This is one of the last batch of "King Arthurs" and was originally fitted with a 6 wheel tender. It is seen here with an 8 wheel tender, which it acquired from a withdrawn "Remembrance" class 4–6–0. May 30th 1959.

A down freight entering Ashford station on the fast line, hauled by class N 2–6–0 No 31407. This is one of the last series of this numerous class, identifiable by the turned in top to the tender side. The bridge under which the train is passing carried the road to Romney Marsh, and was replaced

"Schools" class No 30929 "MALVERN" at the head of the 6.50am (Sundays) Hastings to Ashford train. The large diameter chimney can be observed in this view. June 5th 1960.

An unusual duty for a "Schools" class: No 30922 "MARLBOROUGH" is seen heading westbound through Ashford with a trainload of new cars. April 14th, 1960.

It was rare in the period covered by this album to find a class C 0–6–0 on a main line passenger train. Hither Green based No 31693 is seen here taking water at Ashford on a Charing Cross to Kent Coast train. August 3rd 1960.

"Britannia" class No. 34073 602 SQUADRON taking waters at Ashford on a down main line train June 7th 1960.

The 4.58pm Dover Priory to Tonbridge train arriving at Ashford headed by class D1 4-4-0 No 31246. May 7th 1959.

Class U 2–6–0 No 31807 (one of the class rebuilt from a "River" class 2–6–4T) leaves Ashford with an up main line freight train. It was unusual to find one of this class on this train, which was normally worked by a class N 2–6–0. April 27th 1960.

The Margate portion of a through train from Birkenhead crossing the River Stour on the approach to Chilham, headed by class N 2–6–0 No 31401. June 8th 1957.

Ivatt class 2 2–6–2T No 41311 approaching Ashford on the main line with an up parcels train. June 17th 1959.

"Schools" class 4-4-0 No 30906 "SHERBORNE" leaving Canterbury West with a Margate train. The former engine shed can be seen under the gantry. May 24th 1959.

"Battle of Britain" class No 34086 "219 SQUADRON" is seen here passing Sandling with the down "Golden Arrow". The track seen diverging from the main line towards the camera is the connection with the former Hythe and Sandgate branch. The third rail is in position for the forthcoming electrification. June 4th 1960.

Class 5700 No 4621 brings the "Golden Arrow" down the incline from Folkestone Junction to the harbour, May 10th 1958.

B.R. Standard class 5 4—6—0 No 73084 is seen arriving at Folkestone Junction with an up train. The western portal of Martello tunnel can be seen in the distance, while on the skyline above is the tower, dating from the Napoleonic era, from which the tunnel takes its name. May 10th 1959.

Newly rebuilt "Battle of Britain" class No 34088 "213 SQUADRON" on the turntable at Folkestone Junction, having been turned in readiness for a return run to Victoria, April 24th, 1960.

Former S.E.R. class R 0–6–0Ts (later rebuilt as class R1) first worked on the Folkestone Harbour branch in the closing years of the last century. Nos 31337 and 31107 are seen here assisting at the rear of a boat train leaving the harbour station. September 7th 1956.

The R1s were replaced by W.R. class 5700 0-6-0PTs. Nos 4610 and 4631 are leaving Folkestone Harbour at the head of an up boat-train. May 10th 1959.

Two class 5700 0-6-0PTs No 4610 and 4631 stand outside the shed at Folkestone Junction. April 24th 1960.

"Schools" class No 30929 "MALVERN" is at the head of the 6.50am (Sundays) Hastings to Ashford train near Ruckinge. The large diameter chimney is well seen in this view, June 5th 1960.

The same train, seen here at Ham Street and Orlestone headed by No 30927 "CLIFTON", immaculate in green livery. This train always appeared somewhat incongruous, with a powerful "Schools" class locomotive pulling away only one coach and a few vans. July 31st 1960.

Class H 0-4-4T No 31522 climbing through Orlestone woods with the 10.08am New Romney to Ashford train. The coaching stock presents an interesting variety—an ex-S.E.&C.R. "Birdcage", a Maunsell S.R. corridor third, followed by a 2 coach ex-L.B.&S.C.R. push/pull set. August 5th 1956.

Class Q1 No 33039 drifting down through Ham Street and Orlestone with a Hastings bound freight train. September 4th 1956.

Class L 4–4–0 No 31766 at Ham Street and Orlestone with the 11.38am Hastings to Ashford train. September 4th 1956.

Class Q1 0–6–0 No 33030, piloted by U1 2–6–0 No 31910, climbing through Ham Street and Orlestone with a ballast train. No 31910 was destined to be the last survivor of its class, being withdrawn in 1963. May 3rd 1959.

Class L 4-4-0 No 31781 crossing the Royal Military canal near the village of Warehorne, between Ham Street and Appledore, with the 9.48am Ashford to Hastings train. The coaches are an ex-S.E.&C.R. "Birdcage" set. June 22nd 1957.

B.R. class 2 6–6–2T No.84021 crossing the River Tillingham shortly after leaving Rye with the 9.12am Ashford to Hastings train. September 12th 1959.

Class H No 31543 at Horsmonden with the 9.07am Paddock Wood to Hawkhurst train. This branch closed on June 12th 1961. May 27th 1961.

No 31324 of the same class is at Goudhurst at the rear of the 8.20am Hawkhurst to Paddock Wood train. The coaching stock is Maunsell push/pull set No 609. May 6th 1961.

Class Q 0-6-0 No 30544 passing Eridge with a Tunbridge Wells to Brighton freight train. May 6th 1961.

The 1.50pm Tunbridge Wells West to Eastbourne train arriving at Eridge, double-headed by class Q 0–6–0 No 30534 and 2–6–4T No 80015. September 18th 1961.

Rebuilt "West Country" class 4–6–2 No 34101 "HARTLAND" at Eridge with the 1.55pm Brighton to Victoria train. This locomotive was formerly used on the "Golden Arrow" and the studs used to carry the decorative arrow can be seen on the smoke deflector. September 18th 1961.

Class N 2-6-0 No. 31817 is leaving Eridge with the 9.10am Tonbridge to Brighton train, September 19th 1961

B.R. Standard class 4 2–6–4T No 80154 approaches Eridge with the 12.10pm Tonbridge to Brighton train. The coaching stock is S.R. 8'6" of 1929. September 18th 1961.

The 4.00pm Tunbridge Wells to Oxted push-pull train leaves Groombridge with class H 0-4-4T No 31544 at the rear. The coaches are ex-S.E.&C.R. unit No 659, and its coach nearest the locomotive was the last "Birdcage" in service. September 9th 1961

The same train, having passed the camera, is caught in sunlight soon after leaving Groombridge. September 9th 1961.

Class N 2-6-0 No 31863 leaving Groombridge with the 3.10pm Tonbridge to Brighton train, September 18th 1961.

B.R. class 4 2–6–4T No 80017 approaches Groombridge with the 2.45pm Eastbourne to Tunbridge Wells West train. April 15th 1961.

Locomotive No. 31876 *Maunsell N Class* at Groombridge Station, on an Eastbourne–Bexhill train, 21 September 1961.

The 11.00am Tunbridge Wells to Oxted train leaves Groombridge on a sunny morning hauled by class H No 31533. June 9th 1962.

B.R. class 4 2–6–4T No 80145 is joining the Tunbridge Wells to Eridge line at Groombridge, heading the 9.08am Victoria to Tunbridge Wells West